DUMB BRITAIN

PRIVATE EYE

Illustrated by Grizelda

Published in Great Britain by
Private Eye Productions Ltd, 6 Carlisle Street,
London W1D 3BN

©2001 Pressdram Ltd

ISBN 1 901784 24
Compiled by Paul Vickers
Designed by Bridget Tisdall
Printed in England by Ebenezer Baylis & Son Ltd,
Worcester
2 4 6 8 10 9 7 5 3 1

THE ANIMAL KINGDOM

Robinson: Which herb is renowned for its stimulating effect on cats?
Contestant: Caffeine

The Weakest Link

Les Dennis: Name a bird that can also be a man's name.
Contestant: Chicken

Family Fortunes

Eamonn Holmes: How many legs does a lobster have?
Contestant: *It doesn't*

National Lottery Jet Set

Judy Finnegan: What kind of a creature is a halibut?
Contestant: *A bird*
Finnegan: Try again.
Contestant: *A ferret*

Midday Money

Robinson: Mice, rats and gerbils belong to what family of animals?
Contestant: Reptiles

The Weakest Link

DJ: Which animal does cashmere come from?
Contestant: The Afghan hound

BBC Radio Nottingham

Robinson: In nature, what is a hornbeam?
Contestant: A shaft of light

The Weakest Link

Chris Tarrant: Which of these is not a flat fish?
    A: Mackerel
    B: Dover Sole
    C: Halibut
    D: Plaice
Contestant: No, we'll take the £8,000 please

'Millionaire'

Robinson: In nature, which animals make both dams and lodges?
Contestant: Sheep

The Weakest Link

Robinson: In nature, what name is given to a colony of ants?
Contestant: *A hive*

The Weakest Link

Robinson: In the animal kingdom, if a leopard is born entirely black, what do we call it?
Contestant: *A black leopard*

The Weakest Link

Robinson: In the animal kingdom, what 'C' is a large North American reindeer?
Nicholas Parsons: *A moose*

The Weakest Link

Robinson: In the animal kingdom, what kind of animal is a 'natterjack'?
Contestant: *An Aardvark*

The Weakest Link

Robinson: What 'S' is a small, insect-eating mammal with a long pointed snout?
Contestant: *A serpent*

The Weakest Link

Richard Madeley: What kind of animal
   do equestrians ride?
Contestant: Fish

Midday Money

Robinson: What is the only marsupial to live in
   America?
Contestant: Dolphins

The Weakest Link

Robinson: What is the correct name for the Australian wild dog?
Contestant: *The Dingbat*

The Weakest Link

Robinson: In the animal kingdom, what is a John Dory?
Contestant: *A rabbit*

The Weakest Link

Robinson: What name is given to a male horse that has been castrated?
Contestant: *A stallion*

The Weakest Link

Robinson: Which bird gives its name to a straight-legged marching step?
Contestant: *The cuckoo*

The Weakest Link

Richard Madeley: Where do rabbits live?
Contestant: *In a hutch*

Midday Money

LITERATURE
● ● ● ● ● ● ● ● ● ●

John Leslie: On which street did Sherlock
   Holmes live?
Contestant: Er…
Leslie: He makes bread…
Contestant: Er…
Leslie: …he makes cakes…
Contestant: Kipling Street?

Midday Money

Robinson: Which famous poet wrote these
   lines: "If I die think only this of me / That
   there's some corner of a foreign field that
   is forever England"?
Wendy Richard: *Byron*

Celebrity Weakest Link

Steve Wright: Which American writer wrote
   the novels *Of Mice and Men* and *The
   Grapes of Wrath*?
Contestant: *Acker Bilk*

Steve Wright Show

Robinson: In which century did William Wordsworth become the Poet Laureate?
Contestant: The 20th

The Weakest Link

Robinson: By what name is the author Eric Blair better known?
Contestant: Frederick Forsyth

The Weakest Link

Robinson: Complete the title of this Oliver Goldsmith novel: The Vicar Of…
Contestant: *Dibley*

William G. Stewart: In the novel and film, what is Howard's End?
Contestant: *A boatyard*

Robinson: The book Three Men in a Boat by Jerome K. Jerome was set on which river?
Contestant: *The Mississippi*

Robinson: Which 1991 John Grisham novel was turned into a film starring Tom Cruise?
Contestant: *The 39 Steps*

Robinson: What nationality was the philosopher Jean Paul Sartre?
Contestant: *Italian*

Robinson: In Alice in Wonderland, which creature does the Mad Hatter pour tea onto to wake him up?
Contestant: A dog

Robinson: In literature, The Knight's Tale and The Nun's Priest Tale are both in which collection of tales by Geoffrey Chaucer?
Wendy Richard: The Miller's Tale

Robinson: In literature – the poet Philip Larkin was born in what century?
Contestant: The 17th

Ulrika Jonsson: Who wrote Lord of the Rings?
Contestant: Enid Blyton

Robinson: For which book did Salman Rushdie win the Booker prize?
Contestant: The Wind in the Willows.

Chris Tarrant: In the science-fiction novel 'The Day Of The Triffids', what are the triffids?

    A: Plants
    B: Wolves
    C: Dinosaurs
    D: Fish

Contestant: *I'm going to phone a friend, Chris*

                   'Millionaire'

Robinson: Dorothy Wordsworth was the sister of which English Romantic poet?
Contestant: *Robert Wordsworth*

The Weakest Link

Judy Finnegan: Which company created The Jungle Book, The Aristocats and The Lion King?
Contestant: *Rudyard Kipling*

Midday Money

Robinson: Complete the title of this well-known children's novel by Arthur Ransome: Swallows and...
Contestant: *Butterflies*

The Weakest Link

William G. Stewart: Which broadcaster links the following – 'Home Truths' on Radio Four, the family album column in the Radio Times and the 'Late Night Sessions' on Radio One?
Contestant: *Evelyn Waugh*

Fifteen-To-One

Robinson: In the children's novel, what kind of animal is Tarka?
Contestant: *A seal*

The Weakest Link

Les Dennis: Name someone associated with Robinson Crusoe...
Contestant: *Peter Pan*

Family Fortunes

Robinson: Which author created the fictional character Bilbo Baggins?
Contestant: Charles Dickens

Robinson: The aviator Biggles was created by which author?
Contestant: G. K. Chesterton

Robinson: Which Conservative politician wrote the novel Lord Collingsby?
Contestant: Lord Archer

Chris Tarrant: Who wrote the poem Paradise Lost?
       A: Alexander Pope
       B: Chaucer
       C: Wilfred Owne
       D: Milton
Contestant: No idea – not even a guess

POPULAR MUSIC
● ● ● ● ● ● ● ● ● ● ● ● ● ●

Judy Finnegan: What are the Christian names
  of The Beatles?
Contestant: Pass

Midday Money

Robinson: Which group provided the
  soundtrack for Saturday Night Fever?
Contestant: Grease

The Weakest Link

Robinson: Which musician famous for playing
  the piano honky-tonk style died last year?
Contestant: Elton John

The Weakest Link

John Leslie: The pop star Mick Jagger is
  married to which famous supermodel?
Contestant: Er...
Leslie: You'll find one in a house...
Contestant: Bianca!

Midday Money

Richard Madeley: Who sang 'New York, New York' and 'Chicago'?
Contestant: Er...
Madeley: His nickname was 'Old Blue Eyes'
Contestant: I don't know

Midday Money

CLASSICAL MUSIC
● ● ● ● ● ● ● ● ● ● ● ● ● ●

Robinson: Which British composer took the music for Land of Hope And Glory from his Pomp and Circumstance marches?
Contestant: *Tchaikovsky*

The Weakest Link

Chris Tarrant: What nationality was the composer Ludwig van Beethoven?
Audience: *Polish (21%)*
English (2%)

'Millionaire' – ask the audience

Robinson: What was the nationality of the composer Sir Edward Elgar?
Contestant: *Norwegian*

The Weakest Link

Richard Madeley: Piano, trombone and clarinet are all types of what?
Contestant: *Wind instrument*

Midday Money

Robinson: What nationality were the
   composers Berlioz and Ravel?
Contestant: Austrian

The Weakest Link

Eamonn Holmes: Who wrote the 1812
   Overture?
Contestant: Beethoven

National Lottery Jet Set

Robinson: In classical music, what 'P' was the
   composer of Peter and the Wolf?
Contestant: Puccini

The Weakest Link

Robinson: In an orchestra, the leader normally
   plays which instrument?
Contestant: The triangle

The Weakest Link

Eamonn Holmes: How many symphonies did
   Beethoven write?
Contestant: 62

Playing for Time

Robinson: The first act of which Gibert and
   Sullivan opera is set in Venice?
Contestant: *The Pirates of Penzance*

The Weakest Link

Robinson: Which Verdi opera is based on the Shakespeare play The Merrie Wives of Windsor?
Contestant: Aïda

The Weakest Link

Robinson: In music, what was the first name of the German composer Bach, who was born in 1685?
Contestant: Edward

The Weakest Link

Robinson: In which century was the Austrian composer Wolfgang Amadeus Mozart born?
Contestant: The Fifteenth

The Weakest Link

John Leslie: Tenor, baritone, falsetto are all types of what?
Contestant: Pass

Midday Money

THE THEATRE
• • • • • • • • • • •

Robinson: Who wrote Cat on a Hot Tin Roof?
Contestant: *Dr Seuss*

The Weakest Link

Ulrika Jonsson: Shakespeare: in *A Midsummer Night's Dream*, which character assumed the head of an ass?
Contestant: *Macbeth*

Dog Eat Dog

Robinson: Complete the title of the well-known play, The Iceman…
Contestant: *Melts*

The Weakest Link

John Leslie: Who wrote Jesus Christ Superstar!
Contestant: *Er…*
Leslie: You know… Joseph…
Contestant: *Er… Joseph?*
Leslie: No, I can't give you that

Midday Money

Robinson: Which English actor played the part of Captain Jean Luc Piccard in the TV series 'Star Trek: The Next Generation'?
Contestant: *Sir John Gielgud*

The Weakest Link

Robinson: Who said: "To err is human, to forgive, divine"?
Contestant: James Shakespeare

Chris Tarrant: Which of these is the title of a Shakespeare play?
    A. As You Like It
    B. As You Love It
    C. As You Wish It
    D. As You Want It
Contestant: Er... I don't know, Chris. Can I phone a friend?

Robinson: In theatre, which 'w' is the off-stage area on either side of the stage?
Contestant: The Grand Opera House in Sydney

Robinson: Duncan was the King of Scotland in which Shakespeare play?
Contestant: Hamlet

Steve Allan: What is the name of the West End show that starred Michael Crawford and featured him as the founder of the Greatest Show on Earth?

Contestant: Barbie

Steve Allan on LBC

Gay Byrne: In the play Julius Caesar by William Shakespeare, complete the next line 'Friends, Romans, Countrymen, lend me...'

Contestant: A few bob

'Millionaire' – Irish version

ART
● ● ●

Robinson: What modelling material is it which is translated from the French for 'chewed paper'?
Contestant: Lego

Robinson: Prince Charles described the extension to which building as "a monstrous carbuncle"?
Contestant: Windsor Castle

Robinson: In which movement in art are the painters Cezanne and Monet associated?
Contestant: The Renaissance

Chris Tarrant: Salvador Dali was associated with which art movement?
Audience: Impressionism (25%)

Robinson: Was the painter Francis Bacon born in the 18th, 19th or 20th centuries?
Contestant: The Eighteenth

Robinson: Which artist's work between 1901 and mid-1904 is referred to as his 'blue period'?
Contestant: Gainsborough

William G. Stewart: The novelist Cervantes, the painter Dali and the composer De Falla are of which nationality?
Contestant: German

Robinson: Famous for his Sistine Chapel, Bounarroti was which artist's second name?
Contestant: Giotto

HAUTE COUTURE
••••••••••••••

Robinson: What sort of women's fashion was known as a 'baby doll'?
Contestant: Trousers

The Weakest Link

Judy Finnegan: What is the name of the famous checked pattern worn by Scotsmen?
Contestant: The kilt

Midday Money

Robinson: In clothing, a stovepipe is a type of what?
Alice Beer: Trouser

Celebrity Weakest Link

Nadia Sawalha: Which profession is associated with Grub Street, London?
Contestant: Tailoring

It's Not the Answer

Robinson: In fashion, what is the French for "ready to wear"?
Contestant: Pret à Manger

The Weakest Link

THE HUMAN BODY
• • • • • • • • • • •

Robinson: In what part of
the human body
would you find the
femur?
Contestant: The ears

The Weakest Link

Les Dennis: Name something easy to do
forwards but difficult to do backwards.
Contestant: Eating

Family Fortunes

Les Dennis: Name something you can do in the
bath but not in the shower…
Contestant: Wash your feet

Family Fortunes

Robinson: During human ovulation, the egg
cell is released into which tube?
Contestant: The ovary

The Weakest Link

RELIGION
• • • • • • • •

Robinson: Adam and Eve made clothes from
the leaves of which tree?
Contestant: The eucalyptus

The Weakest Link

Richard Madeley: Who betrayed Jesus?
Contestant: Er... pass

Midday Money

Chris Tarrant: Which Gospel occurs first in the
Bible?
> A: Mark?
> B: John?
> C: Matthew?
> D: Luke?

Contestant: I'll ask the audience please, Chris

'Millionaire'

Robinson: In which town was Jesus born?
Contestant: Nazareth

The Weakest Link

Richard Madeley: How many days are there in Lent?
Contestant: 30

William G. Stewart: Who was the Roman Emperor when Jesus was born?
Contestant: Pilate

Robinson: What 'L' is the alternative name for the Devil?
Contestant: Beelzebub

Robinson: Which of the seven deadly sins begins with 'L'?
Contestant: Love

Robinson: The four Gospels of the New Testament are attributed to: Matthew, Mark, John and who?
Contestant: Joe

Robinson: In the Bible, whose army was Goliath with when he was defeated by David?
Contestant: *Oliver's*

The Weakest Link

33

Richard Madeley: Which religion do you practice in a synagogue?
Contestant: Pass

Midday Money

Judy Finnegan: Who is the first man named in the Bible?
Contestant: God. Er no... Jesus

Midday Money

Robinson: In which type of building will you find an apse, a nave and an ambulatory?
Contestant: A hospital

The Weakest Link

Robinson: What is the Holy Grail?
Contestant: The urn where Jesus' ashes are kept

The Weakest Link

William G. Stewart: In the Bible, who said: "Henceforth all generations will call me blessed"?
Contestant: Jesus

Fifteen-To-One

CINEMA
•••••••

Robinson: Which Australian born actor starred in the 1933 version of Mutiny on the Bounty?
Contestant: Mel Gibson

The Weakest Link

Robinson: Which legendary film maker directed 'The Greatest Show on Earth' and 'The Ten Commandments'?
Vanessa Feltz: Sam Peckinpah

Celebrity Weakest Link

Richard Madeley: What nationality is the actor Anthony Hopkins?
Contestant: Er...
Madeley: Look you Boyo...We'll keep a welcome in the hillsides...
Contestant: Scottish
Madeley: No! How green was my valley...
Contestant: Irish

Midday Money

Chris Tarrant: Which character does Bela
　　Lugosi famously play?
Audience: Tarzan (9%)

'Millionaire' – ask the audience

Robinson: Which 1954 film starred Judy
　　Garland and then Barbara Streisand in
　　1976 when it was re-made?
Contestant: The Wizard of Oz

The Weakest Link

Gaynor Faye: Which actress starred in Sleepless in Seattle and When Harry Met Sally?
Contestant: *Tom Hanks*

Robinson: Which actor played the gin-drinking boatman in the 1951 film 'The African Queen'?
Contestant: *Bing Crosby*

Robinson: In which genre of film would you most associate Gary Cooper?
Contestant: *Slapstick*

Richard Madeley: Michael Douglas's dad is called…?
Contestant: *Michael Douglas*

Steve Wright: Which of the Marx brothers didn't speak?
Contestant: *Karl*

SPORT
• • • • • •

Richard Madeley: What is the name of the
    court on which the men's final is played at
    Wimbledon?
Contestant: *Earls Court*
Madeley: No, no, I'll help you. It's, er, slap in
    the middle… at the dead…
Contestant: *End*

Midday Money

**William G.
    Stewart:**
Which
measure, equal
to one eighth
of a mile, is
mainly used in
horse racing?
Contestant: *A
    fathom*
    Fifteen-To-One

Robinson: In what year of the 90s did badminton and basketball become Olympic medal sports?
Contestant: 1984

The Weakest Link

Robinson: Which cricketer was nicknamed 'fiery Fred'?
Contestant: Fred Botham

The Weakest Link

Nadia Sawalha: Who did Joe Louis beat in the last two defences of his title?
Contestant: Frank Bruno

It's Not The Answer

Robinson: In darts, how many points would you get if you hit double 18, 6 and 2?
Alice Beer: One hundred and eighty

Celebrity Weakest Link

Tommy Boyd: Which famous footballer was killed by lightning on a golf course in 1965?
Contestant: Bob Marley

Talksport

FOREIGN AFFAIRS
● ● ● ● ● ● ● ● ● ● ● ● ● ●

Robinson: Of which African country was
  Canaan Banana the President?
Contestant: Peru

The Weakest Link

Robinson: In what year of the 1990s did
  Saddam Hussein trigger off the Gulf War?
Contestant: 1984

The Weakest Link

Richard Madeley: Name one colour of the
  Italian flag?
Contestant: Blue.
Madeley: Yes! … er, no, try again
Contestant: Mauve… Black… Green…
Madeley: Yes!

Midday Money

Robinson: Who is the president of Iraq?
Contestant: Ehud Barak

The Weakest Link

Robinson: What organisation was established by the signing of the North Atlantic Treaty?
Contestant: *OPEC*

The Weakest Link

Eamonn Holmes: Who coined the term "The Iron Curtain"?
Contestant: *Gorbachev*

National Lottery Jet Set

Robinson: Robert Mugabe is the president of which African country?
Contestant: *Nigeria*

The Weakest Link

Robinson: Oliver Tambo was a leading figure in the history of which country?
Contestant: *Uganda*

The Weakest Link

Robinson: Jomo Kenyatta was the president of which country?
Contestant: *Japan*

The Weakest Link

Chris Tarrant: With which country was the politician Nehru associated with?
Audience: South Africa (19%)
France (3%)

'Millionaire' – ask the audience

Robinson: In which country was Ehud Barak elected as President in 1999?
Contestant: Egypt

The Weakest Link

William G. Stewart: New Zealand has two national anthems. One of them is God Save The Queen. What's the other one?
Contestant: Australia Fair

Fifteen-To-One

Richard Madeley: Who did Britain go to war with over the Falklands?
Contestant: Er...
Madeley: It's a South American country.
Contestant: Iran?

Midday Money

William G. Stewart: What was the name of the island on which Nelson Mandela was imprisoned?
Contestant: Ellis Island

Fifteen-To-One

BRITISH POLITICS
●●●●●●●●●●●●●●●●

Richard Madeley: Who was the prime minister before Tony Blair?
Contestant: Pass

Midday Money

Denise Van Outen: He was a very boring Prime Minister, he lost the last election and his name is a rank in the army...
Tara Palmer-Tomkinson: *Al Gore... no, Bush!*

The Big Breakfast

Eamonn Holmes: Who is the current Secretary of State for Education?
Contestant: Michael Portillo

National Lottery Jet Set

Judy Finnegan: What's the Tory leader's Christian name?
Contestant: Er...
Madeley: You know, Mister Hague?
Contestant: Pass

Midday Money

Chris Tarrant: Which organisation associated closely to the Labour Party advocated gradual social reform within the law?

A: The Fabian Society
B: The 1922 Committee
C: The Chiltern Hundreds
D: The Steering Committee

Contestant: *It's the 1922 Committee, Chris*

'Millioniare'

Judy Finnegan: What do the letters MP stand for?

Contestant: *Minister for Parliament*

Midday Money

Robinson: Which British politician gave the infamous 'rivers of blood' speech in 1968?

Contestant: *Harold Macmillan*

The Weakest Link

Judy Finnegan: Which macho member of the cabinet is sometimes known as 'two Jags'?

Contestant: *Michael Heseltine*

Midday Money

Robinson: What did MPs receive for the first
time in 1911?
Contestant: Guns

The Weakest Link

Eamonn Holmes: Who is the leader of the Liberal Democrats?
Contestant: Oh, I know this one – it's Paddy Ashdown

National Lottery Jet Set

John Leslie: Who is the Foreign Secretary?
Contestant: Ooooh…
Leslie: Small, ginger beard… not a chef but a…
Contestant: Pass

Midday Money

Robinson: In British politics there are three branches of government: the legislature, the executive and the what?
Contestant: The chancellor

The Weakest Link

Robinson: Which British prime minister coined the phrase: 'the pound in your pocket'?
Contestant: Asquith

The Weakest Link

Gaynor Faye: True of false: William Hague is a member of the Labour Party

Contestant: *Blair!*

Faye: Correct

Midday Money

Chris Tarrant: Audience, who is the famous son-in-law of the actor Tony Booth?

Audience: *Paul Gascoigne (1%)*

Martin Clunes (12%)

'Millionaire' – ask the audience

NOT SO DUMB
●●●●●●●●●●●●

William G. Stewart: Charles Moore is the editor of which national daily newspaper?

Contestant: *I'm afraid I don't know*

Fifteen-To-One

AMERICAN POLITICS
● ● ● ● ● ● ● ● ● ● ● ● ● ● ● ●

John Leslie: Who is the President of America?
Contestant: Oh... er... pass

Midday Money

Robinson: Did the American President George
      Bush represent the Democratic or the
      Republican party?
Contestant: The Democrats

The Weakest Link

Robinson: Which US President said: "Read my
      lips – no new taxes" during his campaign in
      1989?
Contestant: Clinton

The Weakest Link

Robinson: What was the name of the housing
      scandal that Bill and Hillary Clinton were
      involved in?
Contestant: Watergate

The Weakest Link

Robinson: Which political scandal was the subject of the film All The President's Men?
Contestant: The Whitewater Affair

Robinson: Which American President famously said: "Ask not what your country can do for you but what you can do for your country"?
Contestant: Roosevelt

Ulrika Jonsson: Which US president was shot in 1981?
Contestant: J.F. Kennedy

Richard Madeley: Who was Bill Clinton's vice president?
Contestant: I don't know
Richard: Come on, he also stood for president himself. You know, Al…
Contestant: Al Jolson

HISTORY
●●●●●●●

Richard: In what year did the Second World
War end?
Contestant: *1918*
Richard: No… try again
Contestant: *1937*

Midday Money

Robinson: Which general led the Allied forces
to victory at El Alamein in 1942
Contestant: *Rommel*

The Weakest Link

William G. Stewart: Who became the
brother-in-law of Henry VIII following his
marriage to Henry's sister Margaret?
Contestant: *Mary Queen of Scots*

Fifteen-To-One

Robinson: What is the Queen Mother's maiden
name?
Contestant: *Tudor*

The Weakest Link

Robinson: Who was the wife of Louis XVI of France?

Contestant: Ann Boleyn

The Weakest Link

Richard Madeley: What was the plot hatched by Guy Fawkes known as?

Contestant: Bonfire Night

Midday Money

Nadia Sawalha: Who was the first man to reach the South Pole?

Contestant: Sir Francis Chichester

It's Not The Answer

Robinson: Which country was caught up in the Cultural Revolution of 1966?

Contestant: India

The Weakest Link

William G. Stewart: What ship picked up survivors of the Titanic?
Contestant: The Lusitania

Robinson: In British history, which Queen celebrated her Diamond Jubilee in 1897?
Contestant: Queen Elizabeth the First

Nadia Sawalha: In which spa town did Marshall Petain set up his government in 1940?
Contestant: Bath

Richard Madeley: True or false: Rasputin the mad monk was American?
Contestant: True

Robinson: In which century was Hadrian's Wall built?
Contestant: The Eighteenth Century

Robinson: Who was the mistress of Admiral Nelson?
Contestant: Josephine

The Weakest Link

William G. Stewart: The bones of the young King Edward V and his brother Richard Duke of York were discovered in the Tower of London. How are they usually referred to?
Contestant: Hansel and Gretel

Fifteen-To-One

Robinson: In history, which leader was responsible for the defeat of Edward II at the Battle of Bannockburn?
Contestant: Napoleon

The Weakest Link

Robinson: In history, at the battle of Waterloo, which general's horse was called Copenhagen?
Contestant: Lord Nelson

The Weakest Link

Richard Madeley: When was the Battle of Hastings?
Contestant: 1866

Robinson: Who was crowned King of England in 1066?
Contestant: Harold

The Weakest Link

Eamonn Holmes: Which famous explorer landed in Australia in 1770?
Contestant: Sir Walter Raleigh

National Lottery Jet Set

Jeremy Paxman: Which South American politician overthrew Allende in a coup...
First contestant: *Ayatollah Khomeini*
Second contestant: *Chile*

University Challenge

Robinson: The name of which Italian, born in 1469 is synonymous with immoral cunning?
Contestant: *Mussolini*

The Weakest Link

Anne Robinson: What French word did Karl Marx use to describe those who oppressed the working class?
Contestant: *Trotskyists*

The Weakest Link

William G. Stewart: In the first successful transatlantic flight, Alcock and Brown took off from Newfoundland. In which country did they land?
Contestant: *Canada*

Fifteen-To-One

Robinson: In America, the Gettysburg Address was made during which war?
Contestant: The Second World War

The Weakest Link

Judy Finnegan: Which country was ruled by Tsars – France or Russia?
Contestant: France

Midday Money

Robinson: Name the first President of the United States
Contestant: Abraham Lincoln

The Weakest Link

Judy Finnegan: Which desert war did Britain take part in 10 years ago today?
Contestant: The Falklands

Midday Money

Richard Madeley [Royal question]: Charles and Edward were children of who?
Contestant: Diana

Midday Money

MILITARY
●●●●●●●●

Robinson: Which Cluedo character has a
    military rank?
Contestant: *Colonel Sanders*

The Weakest Link

Robinson: In the
    US Navy, what
    class of ship
    are the USS
    Enterprise
    and the USS
    Independence?
Contestant:
    Spaceships

The Weakest Link

Chris Tarrant: On which type of transport
    would you find a 'poop deck'?
Audience: *Bicycle (7%)*

Millionaire – ask the audience

PLANT LIFE
• • • • • • • • •

Robinson: What 'L' is the name given to any member of the pea or bean family?
Contestant: *Pod*

Robinson: What is the name for trees that don't shed their leaves in the winter?
Contestant: *Deciduous*

Judy Finnegan: Which fruit is dried to make a prune?
Contestant: *A raisin*

Robinson: In nature, what 'C' is the name given to the furry tufts of flowers carried by trees such as willows and hazels in spring?
Contestant: *Tumbleweed*

Robinson: What colour of the rainbow is also a fruit?
Contestant: A violet

The Weakest Link

Judy Finnegan: A shallot is a type of which vegetable?
Contestant: A carrot

Midday Money

SCIENCE AND TECHNOLOGY

●●●●●●●●●●●●●●●●●●●●●●●●

Richard Madeley: Which is heavier: a ton of feathers or a ton of gold?
Contestant: *Gold*

Midday Money

Robinson: In chemistry, what 'L' when added to acidic solutions turns red, but when added to alkaline solutions turns blue?
Contestant: *Lime*

The Weakest Link

Robinson: What distinguished prize did Albert Einstein win in 1921 for his work in physics?
Contestant: *The Booker Prize*

The Weakest Link

Nadia Sawalha: Who in 1901 originated the quantum theory?
Contestant: *Sir Isaac Newton*

It's Not The Answer

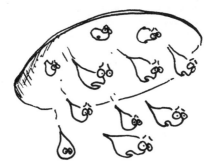

Robinson: In medicine, what 'D' is the separation of liquids through a membrane?
Contestant: Desperation

The Weakest Link

Robinson: In chemistry, what substance is produced by burning hydrogen in air?
Contestant: Oxygen

The Weakest Link

Robinson: What 'B' is a device used to slow down a motor vehicle?
Contestant: *Pass*

Robinson: Which gas comprises 21% of the atmosphere?
Contestant: *Air*

Eamonn Holmes: What was invented in 1926 by John Logie Baird?
Contestant: *Electricity*

Robinson: In maths, if each side of a pyramid is 220m long, how far would you have to walk to go all the way around it?
Contestant: *240 metres*

Robinson: What 'W' is a unit of electrical power?
Contestant: *Webber*

Robinson: Which white substance was used in early gas lighting systems?
Contestant: *Cocaine*

The Weakest Link

Richard Madeley: What was Einstein's name, Albert or Eric?
Contestant: *Eric*

Midday Money

Robinson: Which type of steerable balloon is named after the German count who invented it?
Contestant: Dirigible

Robinson: In science, something that fools the eye is called an optical what?
Contestant: Image

Robinson: Which safety device for miners was invented by Sir Humphrey Davy?
Contestant: Mechanical mining

Robinson: What does a sundial measure?
Contestant: The rays of the sun

Robinson: In geometry, what 'T' is a quadrilateral that only has two parallel sides?
Contestant: A triangle

Robinson: In maths, what 'G' is the degree of the slope of a straight line compared to the horizontal?
Contestant: Gravity

The Weakest Link

William G. Stewart: What is the name of the galaxy in which we live?
Contestant: The earth

Fifteen-To-One

GEOGRAPHY OF BRITAIN
• •

Robinson: In which county is the seaside resort
of Bournemouth?
Contestant: Blackpool

The Weakest Link

Robinson: Mary Arden's house and Ann
Hathaway's cottage are tourist attractions
in which town?
Contestant: Boston

The Weakest Link

DJ: On which Scottish Island is Tallisker
Whisky produced?
Contestant: Er…
DJ: The Isle of…
Contestant: Er… Is it a Glen?
DJ: No, it's an island

Fox FM

Richard Madeley: Leeds, Sheffield and
    Bradford are all cities in which county?
Contestant: I'm Irish, pass

Midday Money

Robinson: The resorts of Paignton and Brixham
    lie on which bay?
Contestant: San Francisco Bay

The Weakest Link

Eamonn Holmes: Which Scottish town recently
    hosted the wedding of Madonna and Guy
    Ritchie?
Contestant: County Donegal

National Lottery Jet Set

William G. Stewart: By what name is the
    113km earthwork built by the Mercian
    King Offa in the 8th century between his
    kingdom and Wales better known?
Contestant: The Appian Way

Fifteen-To-One

EVEN DUMBER THAN BRITAIN
● ●

Jerry Springer: Where is the Eiffel Tower?
US college kid: Paris
Springer: Where is Paris?
Kid: France
Springer: And where is France?
Kid: In England

The Jerry Springer Show

GEOGRAPHY OF THE WORLD
● ●

Robinson: In which country does the Trans-
Siberian railway run?
Contestant: Italy

The Weakest Link

John Leslie: Is the Antarctic a region around
the North or the [shouts] SOUTH!!! Pole
Contestant: The North Pole
Leslie: I do my best

Midday Money

Robinson: What 'B' is the capital of a region of northern Italy and home to one of the oldest universities in Europe?
Contestant: Balti

Robinson: In which country is Quebec?
Contestant: Sudan

Richard Madeley: On which continent is Chile?
Contestant: South Asia

Judy Finnegan: In which American state would you find Los Angeles, San Francisco and Malibu?
Contestant: America
Finnegan: Yes, I'll give you that

Robinson: Strasbourg is in which country?
Contestant: Austria

Eamonn Holmes: Which is the world's largest continent?
Contestant: The Pacific

National Lottery Jet Set

Judy Finnegan: What is the capital of Italy?
Contestant: Pass

Midday Money

John Leslie: The Berlin Wall was demolished in
 which country?
Contestant: Er...
Leslie: East and West came together...
Contestant: Er...
Leslie: It begins with 'G'...
Contestant: Er...
Leslie: No, I can't give you that one

Midday Money

Robinson: What is the capital of Iraq?
Contestant: Islamabad

The Weakest Link

Robinson: Denmark's main airport is near
 which city?
Contestant: Helsinki

The Weakest Link

Robinson: In geography, what two imaginary
 lines are used to locate position on the
 globe?
Contestant: The tropics

The Weakest Link

Richard Madeley: Which ocean is between Britain and America?
Contestant: *The Pacific*

Midday Money

Robinson: Which city is overlooked by Table Mountain?
Contestant: *Rio de Janiero*

The Weakest Link

Robinson: What is the capital of Estonia?
Contestant: *Latvia*

The Weakest Link

Richard Madeley: In which US state will you find Los Angeles, San Francisco and lots of big bears?
Contestant: *Florida*
Madeley: No it's on the other side…
Contestant: *Oh… er…*
Judy Finnegan: 'I wish that they could be da da da da girls!'
Contestant: *New York*

Midday Money

Richard Madeley: Which Danish city is famous for its statue of a mermaid?
Contestant: Denmark

Chris Tarrant: How many islands are there in Japan?
Contestant: That's a tough one, Chris, 'cos Japan has hundreds of little islands.
Tarrant: I don't want to know about the little islands – just the four main islands
Contestant: Er... is the answer three?
Tarrant: No, it's four actually

Robinson: To which country do the Galapagos Islands belong?
Contestant: China

Robinson: Kuala Lumpur is the capital of which country?
Contestant: Mexico

Robinson: Jamaica is in which sea?
Contestant: The Pacific

The Weakest Link

Richard Madeley: In which American city
would you go to the theatre on Broadway?
Contestant: um… pass
Madeley: The Big Apple?
Contestant: [silence]
Madeley: It's a wonderful town
Contestant: [silence]
Madeley: So good they named it twice?
Contestant: er… New York?

Midday Money

Eamonn Holmes: Which American city is
known as 'the windy city'?
Contestant: I think it's Texas

National Lottery Jet Set

Robinson: Which bay does the river Ganges
flow into?
Contestant: Bombay

The Weakest Link

Judy Finnegan: In which country will you find the leaning tower of Pisa?

Contestant: Paris, France

Midday Money

Robinson: Name the imaginary line that runs through the Pacific Ocean along the 180 degree line of longitude?

Contestant: The Maginot Line

The Weakest Link

Robinson: Which South American country has the highest cable car system in the world?

Contestant: Switzerland

The Weakest Link

Judy Finnegan: Gibraltar can be found off which country?
Contestant: Malta

Midday Money

Steve Wright: What is the capital of Australia? And it's not Sydney
Contestant: Sydney

Steve Wright in the Afternoon

Richard Madeley: Name the Spanish island famous for its club scene
Contestant: Spain

Midday Money

Steve Wright: As what is the country previously known as Ceylon now known?
Contestant: Vietnam

Steve Wright in the Afternoon

Judy Finnegan: Where in America is the Golden Gate Bridge?
Contestant: New Orleans

Midday Money

Chris Tarrant: Which of these countries is landlocked?
  Denmark, Belorussia, Chile, Australia?
Audience: Australia (9%)

'Millionaire' – ask the audience

Richard Madeley: What is the capital of Denmark?
Contestant: Er...
Madeley: You know 'Wonderful, wonderful, da da da da...
Contestant: Er... No, pass

Midday Money

Steve Wright: In which African country would you find Mt Kilimanjaro?
Contestant: Nepal

Steve Wright in the Afternoon

Eamonn Holmes: Which is the largest country in South America?
Contestant: Nairobi

National Lottery Jet Set

Robinson: The island of Hispaniola is in which sea?
Contestant: The Mediterranean

The Weakest Link

Steve Wright: What do you call the indigenous people of Australia?
Contestant: Australians

Steve Wright in the Afternoon

Robinson: Tehran is the capital of which country?
Contestant: Iraq

The Weakest Link

Robinson: In mythology, the trident was
   carried by which 'N', the God of the sea?
Contestant: Nero

The Weakest Link

Robinson: In ancient history, Memphis was the
   capital of which country?
Contestant: Tennessee

The Weakest Link

Robinson: What is the name of the huge bronze statue at Rhodes, which was one of the Seven Wonders of the World?
Contestant: The hanging gardens of Babylon

Chris Tarrant: Which of the Seven Wonders of the World was built at Rhodes?
      A: Hanging Gardens of Babylon
      B: Pharos
      C: Temple of Artemis
      D: The Colossus
Contestant: I've been to Rhodes. I think it's Pharos
Tarrant: Why do you think that?
Contestant: Haven't a clue. It sounds vaguely Greek

Robinson: What 'H' was the ancient Italian city destroyed in the same volcanic eruption that destroyed Pompei in 79AD?
Contestant: Hades

Robinson: In Greek mythology, which king fell in love with a statue?
Contestant: Odessy

The Weakest Link

Robinson: In astrology, the Virgin is the symbol of which star sign?
Contestant: Aries

The Weakest Link

Richard Madeley: Who is the Roman God of the sea?
Contestant: Yes

Midday Money

Judy Finnegan: What planet is named after the Roman Goddess of Love?
Contestant (without a moment's hesitation): Neptune

Midday Money

Robinson: What sign of the zodiac is represented by a fish?
Contestant: The Zodiac

The Weakest Link

Robinson: What nationality was Alexander the
Great?
Contestant: Belgian

The Weakest Link

Robinson: Which country continues to lobby
for the return of the Elgin Marbles
currently housed in the British Museum?
Contestant: Egypt

The Weakest Link

THE ENGLISH LANGUAGE
••••••••••••••••••••

Richard Madeley: What is the fifth letter of the
  alphabet?
Contestant: 'F'

Midday Money

Robinson: In spelling, if someone is 'lying' on
  the floor, are they L Y I N G, or
  L I E I N G?
Contestant: L I E I N G

The Weakest Link

William G. Stewart: From the NATO phonetic
  alphabet, Papa, Quebec, Romeo, what
  comes next?
Contestant: Delta

Fifteen-To-One

Richard Madeley: What is the opposite of
  thin?
Contestant: Good

Midday Money

DJ: What is the word meaning stamp collection?
Contestant: *Philanthropist*

BBC Radio Nottingham

Judy Finnegan: Complete the phrase: "Look before you…"
Contestant: *Speak!*

Midday Money

Richard Madeley: According to the proverb, what makes the heart grow fonder?
Contestant: *Love… booze, er… I don't know*

Midday Money

Robinson: Which animal is first in the dictionary?
Contestant: *Man*

The Weakest Link

Roy Waller: What is a comma?
Contestant: *It's a comma*
Waller: Yes, but what's it a part of?
Contestant: *Er… it's when you write*

BBC Radio Norfolk

FOREIGN LANGUAGES
●●●●●●●●●●●●●●●●●●

William G. Stewart: The Latin phrase 'alma mater' literally means bountiful mother. What has it come to mean in everyday use?

Contestant: *Pencil*

Fifteen-To-One

Chris Tarrant: From which language does the word 'chutzpah' derive?

Audience: *French (9%)*
Polynesian (9%)

'Millionaire' – ask the audience

Robinson: What 'C' is the Spanish name given to the conquerors of South America?

Contestant: *Caspian*

The Weakest Link

Judy Finnegan: What would you get if you ordered 'frites' in France?

Contestant: *Pass*

Midday Money

Steve Wright: In England it's called "petrol". What is it called in the United States?
Contestant: Diesel

Steve Wright in the Afternoon

Chris Tarrant: 'Jambon' is the French for which food?
Audience: Jam (11%)

'Millionaire' – ask the audience

Judy Finnegan: What is origami?
Contestant: A herb

Midday Money

MENTAL ARITHMETIC
● ● ● ● ● ● ● ● ● ● ● ● ● ● ● ● ● ●

Robinson: How many hours are there in 3 days?
Contestant: One

The Weakest Link

Judy Finnegan: How many minutes are there in three quarters of an hour?
Contestant: 60

Midday Money

John Leslie: If you were travelling at 25 miles an hour, how far would you go in an hour?
Contestant: 50 miles

Midday Money

Robinson: How many metres make up a kilometre?
Contestant: 700

The Weakest Link

Robinson: How many feet in 1000 yards?
Contestant: 352

The Weakest Link

Richard Madeley: How many wheels on a unicycle?
Contestant: Three

Midday Money

Robinson: In maths, what is 8 times 7?
Contestant: 54

The Weakest Link

Judy Finnegan: How many metres are there in a kilometre?
Contestant: Three

Midday Money

Judy Finnegan: How many cooks spoil the broth?
Contestant: Two

Midday Money

John Leslie: At what time is Midday Money broadcast?
Contestant: Twelve fifteen

Midday Money

COOKING

Gaynor Faye: What would you cook in a wok – no, sorry, what would you use a wok for?
Contestant: Cooking
Faye: Yes!

Midday Money

Robinson: Name the Greek casserole which normally contains lamb, aubergines and potatoes?
Contestant: Paella

The Weakest Link

Richard Madeley: Paella and sangria are mostly enjoyed in which country?
Contestant: Italy

Midday Money

Clive Bull: What breakfast did Goldilocks eat?
Chris Lowry (weatherman): Weetabix
CB: No… a bit more glutinous
CL: Alpen?

Turning the Tables

Richard Madeley: What is the main ingredient of taramasalata?
Contestant: Potatoes

Midday Money

Eamonn Holmes: Which food is the Welsh town of Caerphilly famous for?
Contestant: Cornish pasties

National Lottery Jet Set

NEARLY RIGHT
● ● ● ● ● ● ● ● ● ● ● ●

John Leslie: What is a scallop?
Contestant: A fish
Leslie: Yes!

Midday Money

Judy Finnegan: How many colours in a rainbow?
Contestant: Six?
Madeley: One more?
Contestant: Seven?
Madeley: Yes!

Midday Money

Judy Finnegan: When did the Second World War end?
Contestant: Er... 1947
Finnegan: No, take two away [holds up two fingers]
Contestant: 1945?
Madeley: Correct!

Midday Money

Judy Finnegan: What is a mallard?
Contestant: Er…?
Judy & Richard: Quack, quack, quack, quack…
Contestant: An owl?
Finnegan: Yes! That'll do

Midday Money

Richard Madeley: CO2 is the chemical name
for which gas?
Contestant: Carbon Monoxide
Madeley: Yes! Close enough

Midday Money

Richard Madeley: What is a Finn?
Contestant: On a fish
Richard: That'll do

Midday Money

Robinson: Which cardinal's downfall was
caused by his failure to secure Henry VIII's
divorce?
Contestant: Wesley
Robinson: Correct!

The Weakest Link

JUST TOO DIFFICULT
● ● ● ● ● ● ● ● ● ● ● ● ● ● ● ● ●

Richard Madeley: What do you call the big
    pole that goes up the middle of a ship?
Contestant: *Pass*

Midday Money

Richard Madeley: Who wrote Othello?
Contestant: *No idea*
Richard: He also wrote Hamlet…
Contestant: Pass

Midday Money

Judy Finnegan: What is a red admiral?
***Contestant** (as Judy flaps her arms about): A*
    bird?
Finnegan: It's not a bird but it flaps about…
Contestant: *Pass*

Midday Money

Richard Madeley: Genesis is the first Book in
    the Bible – true or false?
Contestant: *Pass*

Midday Money

Robinson: In maths, what is 9 times 9?
Contestant: Er… [long pause] pass

The Weakest Link

Richard Madeley: What is the Prince of Wales's Christian name?
Contestant: Er…
Madeley: Here's a clue – he was married to Diana
Contestant: Er…
Madeley: It begins with a 'C'
Contestant: No idea

Midday Money

COMMEMORATE THE MARRIAGE OF HRH THINGY & DIANA